Douglas Maxwell

MANCUB

Adapted from the book
The Flight of the Cassowary
By John Levert

OBERON BOOKS
LONDON

WWW.OBERONBOOKS.COM

First published in this adaptation in 2005 by Oberon Books Ltd
521 Caledonian Road, London N7 9RH
Tel: +44 (0) 20 7607 3637 / Fax: +44 (0) 20 7607 3629
e-mail: info@oberonbooks.com
www.oberonbooks.com

A catalogue record for this book is available from the British
Library.

PB ISBN: 9781840024753
E ISBN: 9781849438001

Cover design: Green Light

Mancub was commisioned by Vanishing Point and first performed at the Traverse Theatre, Edinburgh 6 May 2005 with the following cast

Paul J Corrigan

Sandy Grierson

Claire Lamont

Director, Matthew Lenton

Set and Lighting Designer, Kai Fischer

Costume Designer, Becky Minto

Production Manager, Ken Savva

Technical Stage Manager, Maria Bechaalani

Production Photographer, Tim Morozzo

Publicity Design, Greenlight Creative

Set Built by, Stuart Nairn

Project Manager, Severine Wyper

Press and Marketing, Jane Hamilton

Mancub was developed at the Soho Theatre, London in August 2004 with Graham Rooney playing the role of Paul.

I'm waking up.

No.

I'm woken.

Curtains ripped open. Magnifying-glass light.

Covers pulled.

> – c'mon ya sloth. Get up. C'mon. Out of this pigsty.

> – make your mind up, am I a sloth or a pig?

> – neither. You boy are a parasite. On me, on your mother...

On Scotland...on Britain...on The Earth...on The Solar System...

Solar systems. Millions of them. All those specks of dust brought to life in the light of my window.

Maybe each one is a tiny planet? With tiny people and tiny parasites?

Cos even ants have parasites.

So says my book.

So maybe we're all ants?

Dad is for a fact. A tiny creature on a dust speck earth, caught in someone else's light.

I tell him as soon as he goes.

> – if I'm a parasite. You're an ant.

I try not to make eye contact.

First day back after summer is always a pisser don't need any...

– oh look who it isnae! I hope you didn't wake my son up. This is the time of day he gets his rest. Did you get dressed all by yourself? You're a clever boy.

Ho ho ho. He makes himself laugh at least. Ant humour.

– by the way, this time of the day is called *morning* ever heard of it? It lasts until the *afternoon*, that's when you usually get up.

Apparently in ant language that's hilarious.

He turns to his audience and practically takes a bow.

Wee Luke's in danger of choking on his coco pops. He's six and is forgiven.

Mum shakes her head like a TV wife.

This proves we're a happy family.

Not to me.

I take the toast in my gub like a seagull, pat Luke on the head, and I'm out the door.

Outside is Monday, sixth year, exams, and then…

Scotland, Britain, The Earth, the Solar System…

*

I've done absolutely no work over summer. Said I would but didnae.

So instead I've been reading one of Luke's books. It's about animals and I'm doing biology so…you know…I feel better.

Kind of.

The fact that it's a children's book is neither here nor there. It's good. Read it in a day.

Outside my gate is where they skate. They can't really skate, they just flip the board over and fall down. They wear the clothes though.

They're not skating today.

They're a pack on the ground.

> – check it out man! We're burning ants!

The brains of the outfit holds the magnifying glass up to the sun and starts burning a hole in his hat. Which is on his head.

> – it's total agony and everything man!

> – keep going Andrew! It's beautiful.

*

To get to school I have to pass Ken. My neighbour's dog.

Even by dog standards, Ken's an arsehole.

> – roof ark ark ark ark roof roof ark ark ark roof roof roof

All day. All night. He never stops.

His speciality is putting the fear of God into children under the age of eight.

He doesn't bite them. He just frightens them. Ambush style.

Everyday this happens.

I hate him. I don't hate dogs. I love dogs. I just hate Ken.

Ken's a bully. Well. He's like a guidance teacher's *description* of a bully. A stupid coward with no friends who backs off when you stand up to them.

Of course, real bullies love fighting and are surrounded by trainee bullies who also love fighting and they *never* back off.

But Ken's old school.

I pretend to chuck a stone at him and he's gone.

*

I meet Jerry in registration then onto Biology.

Teachers have been splitting us up since Primary Four but we're still laughing.

No one can figure him out. I don't even try.

He's the cleverest by miles but always in trouble.

His own worst enemy.

My best pal.

Two minutes in and Jerry's already in the shit.

Mr Fideles. Fat. Sad. Useless. Blackboard

> – arthropod
>
> – absent

Fideles tries to turn into a teacher. Turns too quick though.

Fools no one.

> – mr Raynor, I'm told you have an aptitude for science, but if you are thrown out by me you'll...em...be hating it. Comprende?
>
> – I'm sorry is this class in English?
>
> – don't test me. Just...you know...don't. Now, what to remember before we get into details, is that all animals are essentially alike. That is, no matter how dissimilar they seem to be, they have more in common with each other than they have in...em...opposition. Got it?

Get it.

Actually, I'd been thinking the same thing all summer.

People are just animals right?

> – we humans are composed of the same cellular structure as the amoeba, the same response systems as the protozoa, the earthworm, the frog or the ape. Got it?

Get it.

    – some of our parts are more highly developed of course, the …em…brain and so on.

    – the arse and so on.

    – …but in essence, we are all related. Related to *all* animals. Somewhere deep down. Got it?

Get it.

I want more.

    – right we're having a test.

Eh? Disaster. It's the first day for Christ sake. No one knows anything. Except Jerry.

    – question…

    – bank.

    – what is…what did you say there?

    – I said bank.

    – you didn't. I know what you really said.

    – I really said bank. It was a joke. You've ruined it now, move on.

    – what is the scientific name for Javaman?

    – pithecanthropus.

    – Nope. Pithecanthropus Erectus.

    – eh?

    – Pithecanthro…

Jerry can go instantly nuts.

    – they're all Erectus you moron! Pithecanthropus Erectus, Sinanthropus Erectus, Australopithecus Erectus.

He can't leave it be.

    – you barely erectus bawbag!

SLAM.

GLASS.

Shuddering door. Shaking teacher.

Quiet.

I immediately look for Karen Cleary. I always do. Funny.

Beautiful. Thinks I'm a fanny.

She's whispering. And texting at the same time.

    – no way, he'll be like totally suspended.

Suspended?

But Mr Fideles' eyes say maybe not.

Animal eyes. More ashamed than scared. A firework dog. A
mouse under glass.

For the rest of the class I watch the shattered hole in the door.

Thinking about it.

Animals are our ancestors right? From apes, from reptiles,
from amphibians we come.

So where is all that stuff? Our inheritance.

Is it like a family? We inherit characteristics from people we've
never met?

Like, Mum says I've got my Grandad's eyes. His sense of
humour too.

But he died before I was born.

So I wonder, where do I really come from?

What animal am I?

**

    – you're a cat!

Oh. Apparently, I'm a cat. Football practice. After school. Mr Sisskind. PE teacher. Nose about to burst through redness. Eyes too, bulging. Wiry arms and legs though. Faster than me.

> – hear me Paul? You're a cat. Sense the movement and spring. Cat! Cat! Cat!

I'm in goals this year. I usually play wide-right but Robbins is out there now and he's good.

I'm not. I'm crap. I really couldn't care less but Sisskind thinks it would break me if I got dropped so goals it is.

> – don't worry about height. Let the morons worry about height. You're clever Paul. The rest of these monkeys are donkeys, but you're clever. That more than makes up for your lack of natural ability.

Tap tap tap. Like a secret now

> – cat.

Sisskind's shitting it about this cup run. We've qualified to the knock-out rounds of the schools cup or something and he's absolutely shitting it.

He's drawn diagrams in his wee pad, voice getting higher, nose getting redder, arms getting wirier.

We're all blank. Except Robins. He understands things like tactics and offside traps. We don't even know how we qualified for the cup, we haven't played a game in eight weeks.

> – I don't want to exaggerate lads, but this is the single most important thing that will ever happen to you in your entire life.

We have a kick around. Robbins is on my side so they're all up the other end. Nothing to do.

Just me and Moose. Central defender. Sisskind's screaming all like

> – Be a nanimal Moose!

> – wa?

– a nanimal!

– wa?

Too late, they're rushing past him. I've got two things to shout

– get back!

Or

– away!

So I choose

– get back!

Wide. Winger. Cross. Crap. Mixup. Miss. Relief. Wrong. Ricochet. Shit. Shot. Dive. Damn. Whistle.

Practise over. Didn't even touch the damn thing.

Trudging back. Moose looks like a nanimal now. Huge heavy head rolling on wide shoulders. Hoofs. Like a bull or…a moose. He moos at me

– my mistake man.

– no worries Moose. Just practise innit.

– aye still but. I let yous doon an that. Moooooooooooo

*

Me and dad are having our nightly fight about milk.

Luke's moaning as usual about his dinner. He hates everything apart from beans. Salad makes him cry worse than falling on concrete. He divides his food into piles and drips tears on them. Mum's doing a deal. Bartering nutrients for colours.

Dad's eyeballing me. He wants to start the game. So do I. It goes like this.

I like milk. I drink milk. Milk's good for you. I need the carton at the table to refill my glass.

This is move one.

      – don't put that on the table. Put it in the fridge where
      it's kept.

And so the game has begun.

Move two is me.

Finish milk. Go to fridge. Bring milk to table. Fill glass. Pause
for dramatic effect. Take milk back to fridge.

      – sit still. You're putting me off my food. All this up and
      down.

Move three is a sigh from me.

Move four. Tricky now. He plays.

      – Luke eat up the nice dinner your mum's made for
      you.

Mmmm interesting. Unusual distracting ploy. Gives me space
to fall into a trap.

Suddenly mum wants in.

      – so did you see any foxy girls at school today Paul eh?
      Har ara ra.

Foxy girls. Jesus Christ. That's a *completely* different game.
She's out her depth. I blank her and try to focus.

But suddenly I find myself at the fridge. I've not been
concentrating. Playing right into his hands.

      – ho! That's a fiver's worth of milk you've drunk
      already the night!

      – s'only three glasses.

      – you'd think we had a cow in there or something.

Pitch invasion.

      – better he's drinking milk than injecting heroin.

Red card for being bizarre. The men play on.

      – I work hard all day putting milk on the table.

– I thought it wasn't meant to go on the table.

– if he wants milk he should buy it himself.

– I havnae got any money but.

Aw naw! What have I done? That my friends, is check mate. Victory to him. There's people on the pitch…

– no money? No money he says! Here's a radical plan then. Get a job. Oh no his lordship feels work's beneath him eh? No time in his busy schedule for employment. Too many videos to watch and computer games to play.

Don't know where he's getting *that* from. Videos? But it's too late for facts. He's already well into a story he's told a thousand times about how he started work three days after he was born. I hear him say

– butcher boy

Butcher boy! What the hell is a butcher boy?

I get good marks at school, I've got okay mates, I play sports, I'm never in trouble. But oh no. I'm a failure, cos I drink milk and I'm not a bloody butcher boy!

I need to be in my room. I hear my mum say

– there's pudding.

But I'm gone. And they argue on.

Feel like I'm burning up about something. Furious about something. Terrified of something.

Luke's pretending to be nervous.

– Paul. Can you do my story?

Yeah.

I read bits of *The Jungle Book*. Not the Disney one that he likes, but the Kipling one he hates.

The bit I read is when Mowgli sees how stupid people are, and how cruel, and he decides the village has to go. He doesn't want to kill folk, just erase their trace. With the wolves and Bagheera and Hathi the elephant they trample it.

– they let the jungle in.

– why?

– cos he likes animals best.

– why?

– he's lived with them. He can speak to them.

– he's a wolf.

– no. He's a boy. Like you.

– you can be a wolf and still look like a boy. You can be both.

– can you? Maybe Dad's an escaped animal and he's been living with us for so long we don't notice eh? Maybe we should give him back to the zoo eh?

– no. Dad's not bad. Not bad like Shere Khan.

– no. Don't suppose he is.

– let the Jungle into this place Hathi! Let in the jungle! Let in the jungle!

✻

First game of the cup run.

One nil to us, two minutes to go. Robbins scored a cracker and he's been crashing at them ever since. He's tanking them single handed.

I've had one save and a backpass clearance from Moose that nearly gave me a bloody thrombo.

Sisskind's losing his shit on the sideline.

– watch your angles! Clear your line! Man on!

God knows what he's on about.

Only now he's flapping like a drowner going down for the third time. It's almost like he's…trying to tell me something.

> – come…out…to…it

There's a rumble in the muck. Posts are, kind of, shuddering. That can only mean…

STAMPEDE!

The world is now boots and teeth and mud and shins and pain and studs and speed.

> – AWAY! I mean, GET BACK!

From a mile to a meter they're here and I'm frozen and here comes the shot!

> – oooooooooo

Time stops. That sound is all around. The players. The crowd. Sisskind. The sky. And now it's leaking out of me into the grass.

> – oooooooooo

The universal sound of a fast moving object hitting someone in the nuts.

I know that letting go'll be worse.

The pain starts high. All lights and brightness. But drops like a roller-coaster.

And in the drop I divide. I feel my body fall but know that the real me flies. The real me is floating away. I can *nearly* grasp it. Nearly understand it. It's nothing to do with school or football or friends or family. It's beyond that. It's an old, old memory, and I've nearly got it…nearly…

> – aaaah

The roller-coaster's jammed and I'm back in the pain.

> – great save wee man!

> – yeeeees!

– moo!

– that was brave play Paul. Brave but clever. You used your head son and now we're in the quarters. This is quite simply the best day of your life. Savour it.

I savour it. Curled in the mud, unable to move. My nuts throbbing like a heart beat.

Girl's trainers. Shit. Karen Cleary.

– that, was like totally funny.

– oh. Haw caw.

– was it sore?

– nawk.

– you all right?

– quack.

No. I don't seem to be all right. I seem to be a duck. I should be all witty and cool but instead I'm lying in the mud holding my nuts and quacking. Someone shouts over. It's Robbins.

– karen. Coming?

– where?

– it's no just football I'm good at by the way. There's other games we can play.

– I don't know how. I'm a beginner.

– I'll teach you. Coming?

– nah. I need a proper coach. So I don't pick up bad habits, like the wrong grip or something. Isn't that right Paul?

– quack.

– exactly. Thanks but no thanks. See you tomorrow Paul. Thanks for the laugh.

– qua qua.

A beginner! If she's a beginner what am I?

✳✳

Back to Jerry's house. To our nest. Playstation paused. Some sounds on and Ping Pong.

He wants a pool-table but his dad says good Jewish people don't play pool.

p-ping p-pong p-ping p-pong

> – it's ridiculous innit. Everything I want he says good Jews don't do. Dye my hair.

p-ping

> – good Jews don't have green hair.

p-pong

> – get a tattoo

p-ping

> – good Jews don't have tattoos

p-pong

> – go and see Eminem.

p-ping

> – good Jews don't like Eminem.

p-pong

> – what about wee Jake? He likes Eminem.

p-ping

> – he's not a good Jew.

p-pong

p-ping p-pong p-ping p-pong

> – did you ask your dad if good Jews are meant to beat up their kids?

p-ping p-ping p-ping p-ping p-ping p-ping p-PONG

    – naw

    – I take it you're not suspended then?

    – nah. Pay for the glass and be a good boy. Same old story innit.

Jerry's Gran comes in. This is a war-zone for her. She hears bombs.

Jerry tortures her.

    – why all this noise?

    – to cover the sound of Paul and I making love Gran I've told you this.

    – what now?

    – we're taking drugs Gran please leave us alone.

    – oh no. No no no drugs. No no.

    – I didn't say drugs Gran I said fugs.

He points at the Playstation as if that explains it.

    – you good boy Paul. Breaking glass in school. This is the worst. His father. Me. I weep for him. Make him stop.

Shrug. Smile. What can you do.

    – I weep!

    – she called me a chodlum today. That's a hoodlum to you goyim. Here Gran, take a chill pill.

He's trying to get his own Gran to eat rat poison pellets.

    – you eat these too Paul?

She's no daft.

    – full of chemicals. Could kill a *rat*.

    – bitch.

– shouldnae do that man. She's old.

– so? She's a hypocrite. They both are. You mention drugs and they freak. But they're the ones all desperate to get me back on the happy pills. How can one drug be good and the other bad?

I pretend I didn't hear the stuff about the happy pills. That was a bad time.

– how come you've got rat poison?

– to kill rats.

Oh yeah. Last year me and Jerry were cutting kindling in his garage and this massive rat wandered out from behind his dad's freezer. Jerry had the axe raised. He was right beside it. But some sort of horror of the rat – some tremendous feeling of revulsion froze him. We watched as the rat crossed between us. Disappearing into the darkness.

It was something about it being a rat. And in the garage, not the house. It wasn't a threat. It wasn't trapped.

It was just something repulsive. Something you let slip away.

– if you've got rats you should get a cat.

p-ping

– good Jews are allergic to cats.

p-pong

***

I'm agitated. That's how they describe birds when a storm's coming.

Agitated.

It's not mysterious. It's air pressure. A change in the pressure makes it hard for them to fly.

That's how I feel. Pressure's dropping. Can't move right. Storm's coming.

It's bad from the bell. Wee first years fall to the ground holding their nuts. Laugh and repeat.

English. Mr Wells. Cool. Usually. Talks pubs on Friday, football on Monday. Music on when you come in. Rips the piss. Only now it's me that's getting it.

Normally it's a scoosh. Compare poems. Line by line. On one hand this, the other hand that, in conclusion they're the same but different. The one thing you can never do is say that the poet is wrong.

– the poet is wrong.

Me by the board. Wells on a desk. Head in hands.

– Paul are you being *deliberately* dim? It's poetic *license*.

– aye but it's not right. You can't say a eagle closes its eyes when it flies. Even if it could it wouldnae. It has to stay absolutely alert.

– *look* though. He's saying 'as *if* the eagle'. The *simile* doesn't *rely* on accuracy.

– it's not the way things are but.

– the *poetic* eagle *changes* the way we *view* the real eagle.

– the poetic eagle wouldn't last a minute as a real eagle.

– well it's lasted a hundred years as a poetic one! Sit down you're doing my Jesusing head in.

Blushing.

– I think I get Paul. Like, if the metaphor's not accurate, the poem suffers cos the connections the poet's making don't work.

– well Karen if you *get* Paul you can have him. Do us *all* a favour.

And we laugh. This is sixth year. We're all adults. Except me.

I want to burst into tears and jump to my death from the window. But I don't.

21

Instead, I go to Biology. Which is the same but different.

> – you misunderstand Paul. In an insect's brain the reception of stimulus and response are…you know… the same thing. Get it?

No.

> – I mean if a fly sees something coming, it takes off. It doesn't think about taking off. It just…you know…does it. Get it?

Apparently not.

Jerry says something under his breath that I don't hear. Karen laughs. More death for me.

> – you can't say a bee *feels* threatened, or *feels* cold, or *feels* hot. Its receptors trigger various degrees of electrical energy to its nerve centre and the bees automatically beat their wings faster to lower the temperature of the hive.

> – so can we say that humans *feel* bored?

Walking home about 19 yards behind Karen. Watching every step. Every wiggle. Imagining the fabric around her body. Trying to remember her smell. Get it? Got it.

How do folk ask folk out? It's a mystery.

I can't speak to her face to face. That's insanity.

I can't phone her. That'd be worse. I can just imagine her

> – guess which little fanny phoned me last night? I was like, no way man.

But it must happen somehow. People have girlfriends. Some people even have sex. They must do, I've seen it on TV.

She's surrounded by guys as always.

It reminds me of birds.

Male birds can only attract a female by showing off. Same as us. This school is an adolescent aviary.

The girls watch as we bump bellies and hop.

We have our crowing cockerels, our singing thrushes, our mocking mocking birds, a whole flock of us stomping the ground as the girls chew gum and send text messages.

I don't want any of that. I want to be an eagle. They don't dance or fight to get attention. They just circle, higher and higher, until they're a speck. Then they fold and plummet to the ground. Eyes wide open.

Faster faster faster faster

Closer closer closer closer

And just before they smash into the ground...wings...land ... silent.

That would impress her. If I was an eagle.

***

We've been waiting for this game. Scared stiff.

> – don't let them spook you lads. You're as good as they are. Difficult territory. Get tough. Be animals.

How are they going to spook us I wonder. I watch the green turn grey from the mini bus window. This game is in the city. Not in the bright lights and megastores that we think it to be, but in a scheme.

The houses look sodden. The shops are battered closed. Beaten shut. Litter and kids roll the streets. Everyone looks drunk and cold. Cold and old. The dogs look guilty. No one can see me.

They're going to be hard this team. Harder than us. We're from a wee place.

Sisskind is doing the pep talk up and down the bus.

> – get tough Marino! Get tough Joey! Robbins! Paul... use your head. Get tough...em...you there.

Immediately there are differences.

First off, no one cares. A van full of footballers, a big news cup run, a schools event, but no one cares. No one is really here to watch, except a couple of our lot. This game has nothing to do with life. We're a joke here with our strips and formations and pre-match nerves. Wee neds chuck stuff and shout.

And then. Something. Else. Oh. Get it. Not one of their players is white. Not one.

And this is what they meant. Couldn't say it. Couldn't even *hint* it. But this is what they meant.

– don't let them spook you lads.

Colour. Don't let colour spook you. Morons. But guess what? It does.

Not the colour of the players though. The colour of the bloody pitch.

This pitch is not green. This pitch is orange. Hard packed lucozade dust.

– what the hell is this?

Immediately though I feel it. I'm *better* in the dust. Maybe I'm a desert animal.

Throw myself at charging feet, relish the pain, gather the ball.

Spring for crosses. Safe to gather. But I PUNCH.

Point blank. BAM.

– AWAY!

Another. Chip. Back back back tip. Corner. I'm out. Grab from a forehead and sweep it to feet.

Where's Jerry? No doubt he'd say something funny about the way Moose apologises for every late tackle.

– my mistake man.

Is Jerry here?

Robbins is our Judas Steer. That's a type of bull that leads the other cattle to the slaughter.

Cos as soon as he touches it, he's surrounded, kicked, pulled and shouldered. But somehow he stays alive. Dragging their defenders out of position, opening up space, waiting for a...

Backheel to Joey, miles out, shuts his eyes, toes it, top corner, GOAL.

Joey's a hero!

Sisskind jumps. So does Moose. So do I.

Half time on the bus. Sisskind can't contain it.

> – they cannae take it. They're no used to the toughness. Maybe they should be playing cricket eh? Ha! Stay tough!

I feel like I'm on the wrong bus. Press my forehead against the glass and tune him out.

Jerry is here. I see him. Standing with Karen. Some other guys. Asian guys. They're laughing. He must have come in his dad's car.

They're miles away.

Second half. Things are heavier. Difficult. Slow. This is no game. No. This is a re-enactment of How War Started. Two manlike gorilla teams of different shade, pushing a boulder into territory.

They have it. We do. They do. We have it.

Hack after hack. Punt into punt.

But in the end it just stops. One nil. We're through. Some people are happy.

My legs are covered in dust. Hard to make it over to where Jerry was.

Is that Jerry? Is. That.

Shit.

No.

Jerry's gone. These guys are. Neds. Casuals my dad says. Loose dirty white trackies. Wrong caps. Wrong colours. Shaky wrong fingers.

Stop walking. Where am I going? Turn round! Shit.

I'm among them now. Smell the fags and the plastic jewellery. They seem ancient. Hungry eyes suddenly alerted to the fact that I'm standing among them. Glassy narrow stares.

These guys have real written all over them. But there's something fake too that makes me fume. Their faces so hard the only place voice can escape is through the nose in a

     – nnnnnawwwwweeeayyyman

Whine. They're whining at me. Touching me. Where is everyone?

     – checkeet oot man.

     – gie's yer boots an at.

     – uck yooo looking it ya daftee

     – gie's yer boots a sayes

     – gonna pish himsell look. Heehehehhe

     – hink yer hard or sumin

I'm a wee boy. Picked on. Tiny. Dying. Nearly. Nearly crying.

This is it.

This is…

But here comes…

Something…

Another me. A way out. That memory again.

The

Rat

And

Now

I

Make

A

Leap

Suddenly

I'm

something about being a rat.

I'm

something repulsive.

I'm

something you let slip away.

I am

a rat.

Not one of them raise a hand. They're horrified. They
disappear.

It's not pleasant to make yourself into a rat. But it's not my
fault. They turned me into to this.

Slowly. Slowly. And I'm back. And I'm shaking.

Wait. Hold on. For a minute there…I was a rat. And that's not
particularly normal. Had I walked on four legs? Had they *seen*
a rat?

I don't feel like a rat now. But. I had been one.

I had.

Jerry and Karen are by my side. Looking at me funny. Had
they seen it too? Don't want to bring it up.

– good game man.

– cheers.

– you were brilliant Paul.

– thanks Karen.

– Jerry's been telling me all about you.

– just the embarrassing stuff.

– oh right.

– and it's agreed. You and me are going out.

STUNNED.

Hold on. Maybe I got it wrong.

– like I know you fancy me and I think you're cool so we should try it.

– em em em em

– he means aye.

What what what what

– you can pick where we're going. Saturday. Right.

I'm totally still. Very calm. I'm. Totally freaking out.

– say something ya muppet.

– don't you want to take me out Paul?

I hear a tiny voice.

– yes please.

– cool. Where?

Blank mind. Sweating from unusual places.

– the zoo. We should go to the zoo.

****

The zoo! The bloody *zoo*. What an absolute arsepiece.

It must be about three in the morning. Dad's snoring the walls down. Block that out. Try to remember. Had she laughed in a kind of

> – hey that's a surprising, fun and potentially interesting idea

kind of way. Or was it more

> – this guy is an absolute arsepiece

Whatever. She laughed. Never even asked which zoo. Just walked off. There's only a wee private zoo about an hour away. That'll need planning oh CHRIST. My stomach's boiling up man. I've nothing to wear. I feel sick. This is a mare. How the hell do people *do* this?

I'm not even going there with the old Turning Into A Rat stuff. This is far more worrying. Go to sleep. Sssshhhh. Only now there's a

Roof roof roof roof roof roof roof roof roof roooo rooooooo ow oooo

Ken.

I've had it with him. I'm going to give that dog a piece of

my mind.

He's in his garden.

> – ho! Give it a rest you. First you're attacking wee kids now you're barking at hee haw in the middle of the night. Shut it!

Ken looks at me like I'm crazy. Dogs can do that. Before I know it I'm spilling my guts. I tell him that I'm sick of his behaviour. That I don't hate him but I do find it hard to like a dog with his personality. He should behave normally I tell him. Most dogs would protect wee kids.

So he starts defending himself. Talking about territory and all that.

> – but Ken they're not other dogs though they're wee
> kids. They're *part* of your territory.

So we debate it back and forth and eventually I promise not to
throw stones and he *finally* promises not to ambush toddlers.

> – but they wear me out, relentlessly rushing to and fro.
> It's maddening Paul I swear it is.

> – also I was wondering if you might give the senseless
> barking in the middle of the night a rest. Some of us are
> trying to sleep.

> – senseless barking? Oh Paul you wondrous innocent.
> It's not senseless dear boy. I'm barking at the moon.

Full moon. Bigger than I've ever seen it.

> – why are you barking at it?

> – because it's full

> – so?

> – so that's what one does.

> – but why?

> – because it's full.

I can see there's to be no reasoning with him. He lets me pat
his head. Strangely, I feel I'm being patronised.

> – Paul, Paul, Paul. Let me explain. You see, the moon,
> when full, looks at me.

> – looks at you?

> – precisely. I'm glad you understand. So, as you will no
> doubt conclude, firm, rhythmical barking is the only
> sure way to nip that kind of nonsense in the bud. I
> mean to say, what else can one do?

I look up. The moon *is* looking at us. A great white eye. I can
feel the pressure in its light. Actually I feel like barking. But I
don't.

– why don't you just go inside Ken? Then you wouldn't see it.

– ah. Well. Tricky business. You see, rather embarrassingly, I em, chew the furniture.

– oh. Oh dear.

– yes. It's…it's a very real problem.

And so we sit. Thinking about problems. And finally I go back to bed.

Man. People talk to dogs all the time, that's fine. But dogs talking back?

Is the moon to blame?

Christ.

One of us must be crazy.

＊＊＊＊

Saturday. Zoo day.

I'm supposed to be helping Dad dig a hole in my Gran's garden. To fix her sewage pipe or something. So I tell him I can't. First I say I'm injured then I stutter into the truth. It makes mum's day.

– ooooh a date. A hot date. Wee Paul's going on a hot date with a hot chick. Wooo!

God Almighty. She lives in an American sitcom. I want out of here.

Dad's taking the whole thing personally of course. Huffing in the corner as if this sewage pipe thing was a surprise for my birthday that took him ages to plan.

– well. I think it's convenient that's all.

He seems to think my life revolves around me trying to put something over on him. He thought it was

> – very convenient

when I got food poisoning last year and spent my entire
holiday on the bog.

I'll bet all those teenage suicides are just folk that've been
told they're fake one too many times and they want to do
something that would be just a simple, straightforward act that
no one could quibble about. So up goes the noose. Down go
the pills. Of course if I did something like that my dad would
be like

> – oh aye. Very convenient. You happen to kill yourself
> just as the bins are needing taken out.

*

We get the bus out to the zoo and Karen is amazing. I'm
sweating and nervous but she just puts me totally at ease.

> – you're like a bad actor in one of those 'coping with
> adolescence' DVDs. Chill out man.

So I do. She's much cleverer than she is in school. And far
funnier.

She's even talking about animals. I think.

> – it's called anthropomorphism. It's when we give
> human characteristics to animals. Like saying a baby
> tiger is sweet, or foxes are tricky or weasels are weasely.
> They're not. They're just animals.

> – should go the other way eh? People are more like
> animals sometimes eh?

Amazing wit from me there.

We get to the zoo and we're both pretty excited even though
it's a total shithole.

There used to be shows here and even a roller-coaster but it's
all rusted away to skeletons. Now there's just caravans and

dirty brown flamingos and big empty cages with signs telling you what's supposed to be in there.

There's hardly any animals left. Feels like there's been a jailbreak. The only survivors are drugged and mangy. Paying the price.

There's a bone thin lion pacing what looks like a drained swimming pool. He sees straight into my eyes and I shiver. He's a captured king from another world. Deposed and ridiculed. His eyes say

> – where is my power?

I bow to him. Show my allegiance and respect. He nods back, secretly. I hope his army plan a daring raid and he's restored to his throne. Bloodily.

> – this is ace. I haven't been to the zoo since I was wee. What made you think of it?

> – I dunno. I like animals. I've been thinking about them a lot recently. My wee brother, Luke, he likes it here. I suppose all wee kids like zoos.

Exactly at this point a wee brat with ice cream all over his jumper is screaming

> – I hate zoos! I wanna go home!

His mum is trying to distract the tantrum.

> – look at the baby badger Liam. Isn't he cute?

> – look at baby Liam, Karen, isn't he cute?

We talk about baby animals. Why all girls love baby animals, even the ones that are going to grow up to be maneating nightmares.

> – it's obvious Paul. Biology. It's inside us from day one.

> – aye I can see that with wee cuddly ones, but what about baby bats or snakes? Or baby rhinos?

> – as it happens, I'm very attracted to baby rhinos.

She laughs. Suddenly I get a feeling in my stomach. A brilliant shining. I want to show off. This time I let it happen. I stir it up.

Head falls low hunch down heavy eyes now nearsighted skin turns bullet proof grey dirt and snort and grunt and trot to her and here I am.

A

Rhino.

She squeals. She's playing.

This makes me mad.

I lower my head.

But I'm playing too. Veer away. Leaves scatter bump and fall.

Lie back on the grass and let my human self fold out. Feeling the rhino go. Feels good. Not like turning into a rat. This was my doing.

> – oh my God. That was the best rhino impression I've ever seen. For a minute there I thought you actually *were* a rhino. You should go on X Factor Rhinoceros Special.

She gets me. Everything is going to change.

LET US OUT

Stuck here in the roaring. Cars behind whip us right. Cars whip us left. Factory hot fumes whip us and whip us. Wash us up on this bloody traffic island.

The bus stop is just across the duel carriage-way. There is no bridge. Cos this is ecology. This is evolution. Only the strongest survive.

Me and Karen cling. Screwed up against the gusts of traffic and dust. Stranded animals in the middle of the road.

LET US OUT

This started funny but it's been ages now.

We'll never get across. We're roadkill. Bugs on a windshield.

To the drivers we're half imagined, seen for a second then gone.

I hate them. These hellish carnivores. Arrogant bastards all.

This is The Road. The Road rules.

> – you shouldn't be walking breathing living feeling. You should be driving queuing roaring steering. If we kill you so what? This is The Road

Noise and glare blur. I have to

BOLT.

Bolt for the forest on the other side. Don't even look just bolt for the green

Karen screeeeeams.

*

On the bus we're quiet. People usually are when they're travelling home.

She was angry at me running across the road like that. But we've joked about it, so it's okay now I think.

Seeing as it's still early she's asked me back to her bit to watch a DVD.

But that feeling hasn't gone. Even though we made it across and we're on the bus, I still feel that pull.

I want to bolt for the forest.

There's no one home except her big brother who does a crusher handshake and makes a joke about Karen being a prostitute.

– she charges wee ugly guys more you know.

When he goes into the living room he says

– laters.

Which actually makes me feel sorry for him.

Karen's room's huge, with a sofa and a desk and loads of candles and art and gothy stuff.

I can't imagine ever taking Karen back to my house. Luke's the only one I could safely introduce her to.

It feels weird. Formal now.

– how many boys have you had up here?

What an arsehole. Why did I say that? Shut up.

– not that, you know, not that, you know, ne ne nut nut nut.

– chill. Not as many as my brother says.

Oh. Ha ha ha. It's all a great laugh to a man of the world such as myself.

She moves closer. Pulls me to the edge of the couch like we're rehearsing a ceremony. She has a hand on my shoulder.

– should we have a wee kiss then?

– ack

I'm suddenly aware I need the toilet. My body seems to be attempting escape, bit by bit. Sweat from everywhere. Hands shaking. Legs bouncing. Mouth dry. Head dizzy. I really *really* need the toilet man! And, oh good, I'm going to be sick.

Part of me wishes I was Luke's age. Or that I was in Jerry's house playing ping pong away from this adult world.

But that all goes when we kiss. At first I just open and close my mouth like a goldfish.

Gup gup gup.

– close your eyes. Take it easy.

My hand's in her hair. I think. Shaking still. But not stopping.
She's guiding me from miles away.

> – don't think about it. Relax.

Don't think. Don't think. So don't. I don't. Don't think.

Just move. Follow. Don't think.

Shit.

I'm thinking.

I'm thinking about salmon. Leaping up stream, uphill, driving
to its death just to mate. Contradicting waterfalls for something
inexplicable. I feel the deep rhythm of the stream push me
back and call me on. I'm bouncing off stones but on I go.

On. On. On.

Must. Must. Must.

Where are my hands now?

> – calm it

I want to crush myself against this current.

> – Paul.

There is no thought. Just a tendon tightness from hip to heart.
And somewhere way below that. A force now. From hip to
toe. Cuts at angles. Fighting upstream. Adoring the

Puuuuuuuush.

> – PAUL!

I flap. I gasp. Scales ripped on the rocks and drowning in air.

She's awkward on the carpet like a wee lassie. Pulling at her
clothes. Legs bent sorely under her.

Please don't let her be scared.

> – that…wasn't very nice.

Oh. God.

> – sorry. I…I…didn't

> – I know. But I don't do that.

> – I'm sorry. I've never…I don't.

And I realise that no-matter what I say, nothing can stop this. This *has* to happen.

I'm

Crying

And she's here. Same but different.

And I've ruined it. Ruined whatever it is. And the tears won't stop. And I can't leave.

> – sshhhh. Chill Paul. It's all right. It was just too quick know what I mean?

> – I'm sorry.

> – you didn't *do* anything. At least you stopped when I asked. We didn't do anything. Nothing happened.

But this isn't me. I'm not supposed to be here. Crying. Scaring people.

This isn't me.

> – look. It's cool. Don't worry. Don't cry. I'll see you tomorrow right?

> – please…don't tell anyone.

> – don't worry.

Outside and I'm dying.

I'm listening to my breath, finding my heartbeat.

I wish I could slow that beat.

Slow that breath.

Fade away.

****

The rain comes in gusts. Impossible to even look up. So I pace.

The grass has gone to mud.

So I pace.

This is the furthest we've ever got in the cup. Apparently. Sisskind wept in the changing rooms. Eyes red like everything else.

> – RAAAA!

We ra! back.

> – raaa!

Makes no difference to me.

Everyone's here. Crowds huddled in plastic coats. Hard to hear them in the rain. Can't even see the faces.

Maybe I got the idea from Ken. Or from Karen. But what I'm doing is marking out my territory.

Obsessed by it. Terr…i…tory.

The penalty area. The goal line. Are all mine. And that is a fact.

That is true.

An animal doesn't care what happens outside his territory.

Has the game started?

But breach that territory, cross that line and suddenly a songbird can kill a hawk. It's all about boundaries. Penguins have a square meter, Leopards, twenty miles.

But they'll die for it. Lions roar round the edges. Bluebirds tweet. But it's a roar to them. It means

> – keep out! This is me! This is mine!

They play. I pace. I have an overwhelming desire to piss out the marks on the mud.

– that's using your head Paul. Pissing all over the place. That's clever play.

Instead I roar.

– ooooooooooorrrrrrrrr

Beat my chest.

– BA! BA!

We're like gorillas now. Our bodies are caked in mud. Only our faces are bare.

But it's not that easy any more. I haven't turned into a gorilla. Not like I turned into a rat or a rhino. Still, in a general way, I'm an animal again.

A sort of universal male animal.

I catch a scent. Sense some kind of bear rear up on his hind legs. Staggering. Dangerous. Close to my boundary. Big.

The territory impulse is simple. Ignore the ball.

Kill the bear.

It's a

SWIPE

That gets him down.

Then another.

– RA!

Another.

– BA!

He's slashed and rolling. Now he knows. I give a victorious

– RA! BA!

Referee's screaming and there are humans fussing all around him.

Robbins is mad, right in my face. Even Moose looks angry.

Them. Us. All around me.

> – wha wha wha?????

Chirp chirp chirp.

A red card right into my eyes flares me up again.

> – RA! BA! This is me! This is mine!
> RAAAAAAAAAAAA!

My roar has silenced the jungle. They step away. Step out of my territory.

And as soon as they do, I'm me again. All that territory stuff has vanished. I see everyone, gawking at me from the other side of the cage.

I see Sisskind. What have I done to him? To them all. My family. Jerry. Karen. Teachers. Strangers. All of them on the other side of my line.

They're all stock still when I push my way through.

**

I put the lights off so I can hear them properly.

Mum and Dad downstairs and fighting. About me. I suppose it must have been really embarrassing for them. Their son attacking someone and screaming and losing the game for the school and whatever else I did.

> – what's he trying to prove? That he's a weirdo or
> something? For God sake, he let the school down, he let
> his team mates down, he let us down

And Scotland…and Britain…The Earth…The Solar System.

> – he's just going through normal teenage stuff. Shouting
> at him's only going to make it worse.

> – normal? Maybe normal for your family. Not mine.
> No one in my family's ever had a breakdown.

> – what's that meant to mean?

– what d'ye think? Your brother. The guy who eats nothing but mushed fruit. No wonder his bloody colon's packed in.

– Paul's not having a breakdown. No one is.

✳✳✳✳

I see Jerry waiting for me at the gates. I haven't come to the phone since, so he's worried. But I can't talk to him.

I'm in control now. I can change whenever I want. So I turn into a fly and buzz past, zigging into a few faces as I fly through corridors. They flap at me, but I'm too fast.

No one can see me.

zzzzzzzzzzzzzzzzzzzzzzzzzzzzzz

In biology Jerry grabs my arm as he sits beside me. As if I'm about to run off.

> – what's up wi you man? You all right. Come round to mine the night. We'll get pissed an that. Right? Talk. Gran can do the stand-up routine that she's written about you taking a flaky at football.

And for Jerry's sake I stay human for the rest of the period.

Fideles is on about frogs.

> – it's like none of you are even…you know…listening. A frog does not *choose* to catch a fly. The frog's eye does. It tells the frog if the fly can be caught. The frog's brain is just the link between eye and tongue. Get it? A connection. A switchboard. Mr Raynor you and I had a long talk about what further outbursts would mean to your academic career!

> – how is this an outburst?

> – right see me after. You're in trouble.

> – eh? All I was going to say's there's a picture on page 281 that explains it.

Fideles like a gunfighter. Eye to eye. Dreading the next move.

Everyone knows the naked pictures are on page 399 so Jerry's for real.

The picture is of a frog that is surrounded by dead flies on strings.

The frog will starve because it doesn't recognise the flies as food.

It hears only what it's told to hear. It sees what it's told to see.

But what if we're just like it? What if all around us is another world?

Invisible things.

Real. Beautiful. Vital. Things.

Things that we don't see cos our receptors have tuned them out.

What if God has strung all the answers out in front of us, and we're starving to death because we don't see them?

**

– good Jews don't drink alcohol. They entertain.

His dad's vodka is on top of the wardrobe.

– we can drink it with orange juice. Half an half innit?

I don't know. Feel better though.

– so have you gone nuts or what? Anything you'd like to share with the group?

I'm just going to tell him.

– I think I'm having an identity crisis or something man.

– you don't know if you're a boy or a girl? Thought so.

> – no. Actually…I don't know if I'm a human or an
> animal.

No laugh. His eyes are somewhere else.

On on on I go on

> – it's. Like. Evolution and that. We're the highest form
> right? But what if that's *all* we are? A collection of
> animal parts? Maybe all the animals we've evolved
> from are still with us, like bacteria in your stomach or a
> virus in your blood?

> – how'd you get steaming so quick man?

> – no. Jerry. Listen. I need your help. I can turn into
> animals. Really.

He tries to laugh, but again, I've ruined something.

We're worlds away from Ping-Pong now.

He asks questions but doesn't want the answers.

Can I do it whenever I want?

p-ping

Can he see me do it?

p-pong

Do I believe I'm actually doing it or is it just a feeling?

p-ping

Is it like being high?

p-pong

Do I mind that he'd invited Karen round?

p –

> – what?

> – she was asking about you. I said to come over. Have a
> party. What? Look it's cool, just don't tell her about the
> animal stuff right. Don't tell anyone. I know what it's

44

like when your head gets messed up, it's...horrible. But don't tell folk. Tell folk and they'll drug you. And then you're finished. You're better out of that team anyway. No offence but you're a shite keeper and they're all fudds.

His Gran has ghosted up at the door.

    – the disgrace!

Me? No. Him. Us.

    – the disgrace! Shame on your father's house.

    – well that's not my fault.

    – the end. You will have to go.

    – remember to breathe Gran. And to talk sense.

    – it'll be cold. He will wander, a young man who is a drunkard.

    – Gran, if you want to stop but can't, try to signal to us somehow.

    – with his breath the breath of a shikker!

She was showing Karen in.

    – I thought you said this was a party.

    – it is. Don't worry about Gran. She's mad. Yes I'm talking about you. Cheeri Bye. C'mon in.

She smiles at me. Not scared. Not angry. A blue sky smile.

    – hiya Paul. Y'all right?

    – yeah.

    – wanted to talk to you.

Jerry's pouring more half and halves when his father's voice stops him dead from walls away.

Can't make out the words but can translate the tone.

    – come here and get your ass kicked.

Jerry thinks about blanking him. But the voice won't stop. He doesn't look at us when he leaves the room.

> – shit. He's in trouble eh? Should we go?

I don't answer. Can't straighten myself out here.

> – I was at the game. I hope it wasn't my fault or something.

I want to tell her that it's all about me – no one else – me me me but...

Don't cry! Don't! Don't! Don't!

> – so what's up?

So I tell her. About the animals. About Ken. About everything.

And she doesn't laugh. She doesn't pity me. She just nods.

She gets me.

> – like the rhino at the zoo?

> – exactly! You can tell them. That I was a rhino! You saw me!

> – yeah. I did. And you were a Rhino. For a minute.

> – and at the game you saw me there too. Everyone did.

> – I couldn't recognise you. You weren't even like a person, you were wild like

> – an animal.

> – I suppose so. No one could take their eyes off you. Like they could see it too.

> – so, what do you think?

> – I think...it's scary.

Upstairs. Jerry and his dad. There's a whiplash in the volume.

Karen and me go quiet. Like tiny creatures waiting for clues to the predator.

It's only a second after Jerry says

> – fuck you

That he hits the floor. We hear him cry out. We hear his dad wade in. His Gran might be pleading. Jerry might be pleading.

I can't breath cos there's blood beat beat beating.

Little gasps of breath. Breathe breathe breathing.

Karen looks scared now.

Now I'm the predator

Bounding through the door

Pounding up the stairs

Catch the scent and adjust

They're in there.

My breath scrapes the fangs infra red eyes snarl on the jaws extend claws

They all freeze when they see me.

Jerry bleeding on the floor his dad above him sweating

breathing holding something his gran sat tears frozen until I say so.

All of them frozen until I say so.

This animal stillness is my doing.

This is the stare before the attack.

One move and I'm triggered. And they all know it. It's primal.

We're born ready for moments like this.

We all react in the same way to wild creatures.

Then Jerry puts his hand out. I notice he's broken a finger.

> – please Paul. Don't. Please.

Karen's here. Goes to him.

It's in the way she touches his face. It's in the way he doesn't look at her. All eyes still on me.

Get it?

Got it.

Before I run for the door I turn on Jerry's dad. Maybe I speak it. Maybe not. But he gets the message.

    – if I wanted to. I could fucking gore you.

Then I'm running.

Just a boy.

Running home.

✳✳✳✳

Can't face going in. So I look for Ken.

    – grrr roof roof ark ak…ak…

    – woah Ken. Ken it's me!

    – oh. Paul. You…I didn't recognise you. I eh ak…ak…
ak…

    – what's wrong?

    – I ak ak ak seem to eaten more than my fair share of
grass. Carpet.

I hear him. Clearly. Not inside my head. But really. His mouth moves. He speaks.

    – Ken? I need your help. I think I'm maybe… going
crazy or something. I…I…could you talk when
someone else is there? To prove it. Once and for all.

    – no. Absolutely not.

– why?

– because they'd try to cure you. But me they'd put to sleep.

*

In through the back door to the kitchen. Mum and dad sitting at the table.

It's got dark but they haven't noticed.

Dad's drinking a beer and wearing a tie. Mum looks scared. Trying not to cry.

Caught in the act.

    – oh hiya son. How are you darling?

Too nice.

    – I'm going to my room.

But I don't. I open the fridge and wait. Looking at milk. Knowing that I've lit us up with buzzing light. Made them realise it's dark in here.

Dad puts his hand on my shoulder and offers me his can.

It's a child's move.

But it's a really *good* move.

And we talk. He's not angry about me losing the match, or hitting that guy. He says he's worried that's all. Mum says that they love me and that growing up is hard. Dad tries a joke about never growing up or something. We all smile with varying degrees of success.

When I tell them about the animals dad has to sigh and get another beer. Mum watches him unblinking. Waiting for him to speak as if he's the one asking for help. He just says

    – Christ.

Quiet enough to make me cry.

Mum cries too. Holding my shoulders.

> – it's just…normal…you get ideas…you've got such an amazing imagination.

Why doesn't dad want to know what I'm trying to prove? Why isn't this convenient?

When he does speak he's serious and calm. His voice is low and steady. He's trying really hard. Unfortunately he makes no sense. You think he's going to come to a point. But he doesn't. He can't. Like two parallel lines receding into infinity.

I'm too passive. I let things happen to me. I try too hard. I'm a perfectionist. I get that from him.

I get too upset when I fail. I think too much and get obsessed with things that aren't important in life. I get that from mum.

I can trust them. They love me. But I can't rely on them forever.

I don't need this. I need him to hold me like I was a baby and whisper a plan. I need him to tell me what to do.

Mum can sense it.

> – there's a therapist that comes to the school. It's totally confidential and the guidance people say he's very good. If you like we can all go. Dad says he'll come with us. It's a normal thing now. Everyone does it.

They've been to the school. Dad is wearing a tie. I can't tell if he looks really old or really young. I can't see his face at all.

And now he seems to be talking about the weather.

> – it's fine. Fine. You'll be okay.

The talk is over.

Luke's in the hall. He's terrified. He's been listening.

I'm his big brother. So there's a twist in the order. Doesn't it get better when people get older?

    – is it cos you like animals?

    – it's fine. Fine. I'll be okay.

    – but you like animals too much.

    – I'm fine.

    – mum was crying.

    – I know.

I lift him up to his room. When he asks if it's his fault I burst into tears and he does too. He takes that as a yes. He takes Kipling's *Jungle Book* and throws into mum and dad's bedroom.

    – gone. Now you're better.

There's something glorious about how grand he makes the gesture. It makes me laugh. Makes us laugh. I curl up beside him and fall asleep listening. He's telling me about two birds he saw who were fighting. It was scary he says.

They were just mating. Just living.

It is scary sometimes.

****

The truth is spoken in biology.

Apt really.

Fideles is on a roll.

    – take the pineal gland…

    – said the actress to the bishop!

Jerry looks to me for the laugh. I can't.

    – it's in the brain. The philosopher Descartes thought it
    was the seat of all consciousness. Get it? Mystics gave

it…you know…strange powers. 'The third eye' if you will.

– the winking brown eye, if you will.

This time Fideles just looks at him. The final straw. The class is silent. There's a decision being made. A coward's decision.

> – by the way, I understand we have someone in the class who has managed to focus his third eye on things. Someone whose brain understands mystical connections. A new…em…Saint Francis. Someone who can talk to the animals. Even, I'm told, turn into animals at will! Well, all I can say is, give us a phone when the space ship lands. Heh heh heh. Now, the brain stem…

He didn't even look at me when he said it. But everyone else did.

Because they know already.

There's panic in Jerry's eyes.

There's so much shame in mine.

He told someone.

When the bell goes Jerry's at my shoulder

> – I was asking him for advice, y'know to prove that you'd got it all mixed up, evolution an that, to put you off, y'know, help you, I didn't think he'd bloody announce it.

> – what about the others?

> – I don't know…maybe I…I'm sorry.

The black eye looks sore. His finger's in plaster. But the face isn't familiar.

Karen's here.

> – we just want to help you Paul. We're your pals.

Not anymore. I can see. She pities me.

Every fibre needs to bolt for the forest.

So I move. Let the instinct take over. Pushing through to the double doors.

No.

Arm held back. Pulling me to turn. He looks just like his dad.

> – We were just trying to help.

We. I let my shark eyes look back. Dead cold black heartless.

A shark has to keep moving or it'll die. So I move move move

On on on.

Push push push

Stopped again. One on each arm.

> – you…fucking…you think you're so special. I'm the pariah here. You're the white, middle-class-kid with the steady family.

> – so?

> – so. Why? Why is this happening to *you*? What's so special about *you*?

> – you told them all. To get her.

Karen shakes her head. Doesn't get it. Jerry does.

He's close to my ear now. Making sure I hear it.

He's saying that I don't have a psychological condition.

> – to hear animals is one thing, to turn into animals is another, to see folk as animals is another still…

Karen's pulling at him. She thinks it's getting through to me but it's not.

> – you've misunderstood the basic science of it. Evolution's not the way you imagine it. You don't adapt just because you want to. People aren't made from

layers. Evolution is radiational not linear. You're not part frog. Part snake. Part human.

– it's real though! I can do it. You saw me! Both of you!

– no mate. You need help. You want a friend that listens to all this shit and smiles lovingly without doing anything about it? Get a fucking dog!

Why I say it I don't know. But it's a shriek from down below.

– I'LL FLY! I'LL SHOW YOU I'M REAL! I'LL FLY!

We're outside now.

Scotland…Britain…The Earth…The Solar System…

Me. Karen. Jerry.

And the whole school.

*

It's like a storm suddenly here. Pressure has dropped. The whole aviary's agitated. There's a burnt smell in the air.

My blood in the water.

From the corridors to the classroom, from playground to park, from the gym to the assembly hall. All species are on the hunt. The cry has gone out to the corners of the jungle.

They are united.

I make out some of the laughing faces.

There's Joey, Moose and Robbins. Clapping and singing something about animals.

Robbins doesn't laugh. His hate is pure. It's from the game. Not this.

Moose? Why does that hurt? Why are you here?

Where are the teachers? In their lair.

Now here comes the scuffle. Someone grabs my shirt.

Jerry lashes. He's spitting and punching. Those tears that only come in a fight. His face red. His finger broken.

He's defending me! Fighting them off.

He would save me if he could.

Karen too. She shouts something in the face of a girl leering in.

But I'm pulled away. Surrounded. Ruined.

Jerry's rage is useless against a storm like this.

> – don't cry Paul.

My mum will say.

> – it's fine. Fine. It'll be okay.

HI HI HI

What?

FI FI FI

What?

> – FLY! FLY! FLY! FLY! FLY! FLY! FLY!

And we'll sit on the steps at the back of the house. My dad will have a beer. Luke will have his head on my lap.

Mum will put her arms around me.

Jerry will be there.

And Karen too.

Dad will hold me like a baby and tell me what to do.

Jerry will say something about animals and he'll be joking.

We'll go inside and I'll be waking up.

No.

I'll have woken.

But.

Until then.

I'm running.

I'm running and crying.

Closer and closer stones and fists

I realise.

I don't have any choice in this. Never have.

It's an animal's only thought.

To keep itself alive.

So escape it is.

I spread my wings

I close my eyes

I fly.

****

WWW.OBERONBOOKS.COM

Follow us on www.twitter.com/@oberonbooks
& www.facebook.com/OberonBooksLondon

Printed in the USA
CPSIA information can be obtained
at www.ICGtesting.com
LVHW021003171024
794056LV00004B/1306